Learning Express

Time and Measurement

This book belongs to

Ella

Ello

Previously published as Reading & Math Jumbo Workbook Grade 2, Success With Math Grade 1 & 2
and Summer Express 1-2 & 2-3
by Scholastic Inc.

This edition published by Scholastic Education International (Singapore) Private Limited
A division of Scholastic Inc.

First edition 2013

ISBN 978-981-07-1367-6

Welcome to Learning Express!

Helping your child build essential skills is easy!
These teacher-approved activities have been specially developed to make learning both accessible and enjoyable. On each page, you'll find:

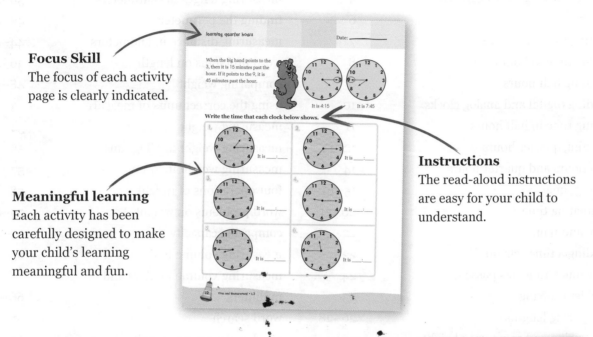

Focus Skill
The focus of each activity page is clearly indicated.

Instructions
The read-aloud instructions are easy for your child to understand.

Meaningful learning
Each activity has been carefully designed to make your child's learning meaningful and fun.

This book also contains:

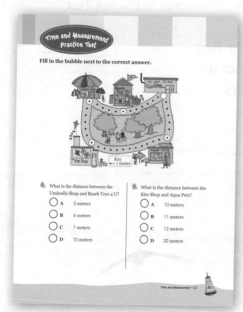

Instant assessment to ensure your child really masters the skills.

Completion certificate to celebrate your child's leap in learning.

Motivational stickers to mark the milestones of your child's learning path.

Contents

Time and Measurement

What time is it? How long is that rope? These are questions your child might ask or be asked. The answers may be important to what he or she does that day. The activities in this section give your child practice with the important concepts of time and measurement.

What to do

Have your child work out the problems on each activity page. Check the answers together. For a quick check, check the answer key at the back of the book.

Keep On Going!

Play 20 questions. Make up questions concerning time or measurement for your child to answer. Have him or her make up questions for you to answer. Ask questions such as: *What time is it? How much taller are you than your friend Gabe?*

Date: _____ ETI a

Look at the time shown on the clock face. Write the time below.

_____3_____ o'clock

_____ o'clock

_____ o'clock

_____ o'clock

_____ o'clock

_____ o'clock

_____ o'clock

_____ o'clock

_____ o'clock

Date: _____

Look at the time shown on the clock face. Write the time below.

__4__ o'clock

or __4__ : __00__

___ o'clock

or ___ : ___

___ o'clock

or ___ : ___

___ o'clock

or ___ : ___

___ o'clock

or ___ : ___

___ o'clock

or ___ : ___

___ o'clock

or ___ : ___

___ o'clock

or ___ : ___

___ o'clock

or ___ : ___

Date: _____

Draw the hands on the clocks to show the correct time.

1.
3:00

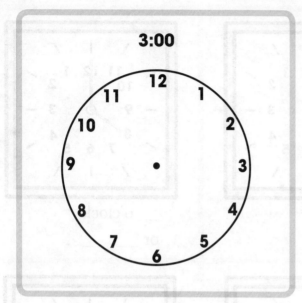

2.
6:00

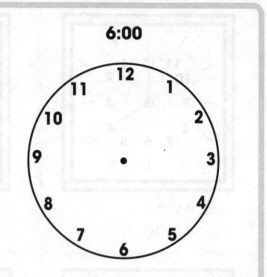

3.
9:00

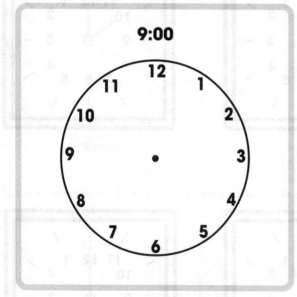

4.
12:00

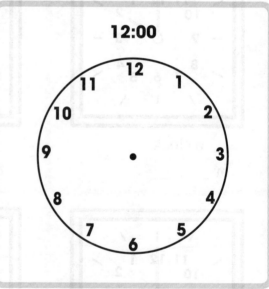

What do you do at 3:00 in the afternoon? Write about it on the lines below.

_____

_____

Date: _____

Look at the time shown on the clock face. Write the time below.

half past _____1_____

half past _____

half past _____

half past _____

half past _____

half past _____

half past _____

half past _____

half past _____

Date: _____

Match the time shown on the analog clocks with the digital clocks.

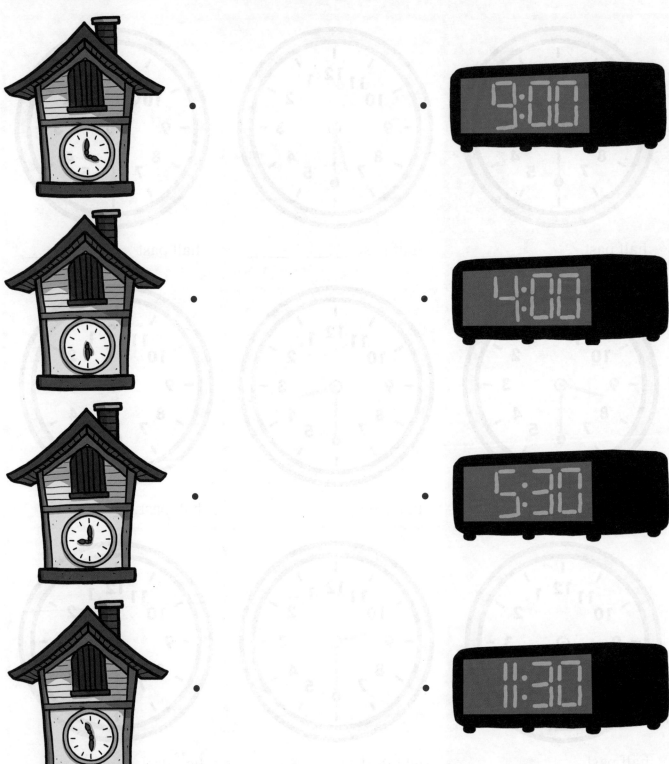

Date: _____

Draw the hands on the clocks to show the correct time.

1.
4:00

2.
4:30

What do you do at 4:00 in the afternoon? Write about it on the lines below.

_____

_____

3.
6:00

4.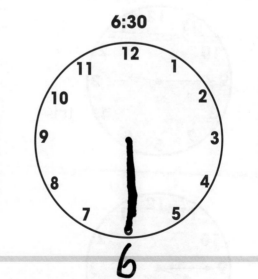
6:30

What do you do at 6:00 in the evening? Write about it on the lines below.

_____

_____

Date: _____

When the big hand points to the 3, then it is 15 minutes past the hour. If it points to the 9, it is 45 minutes past the hour.

It is 4:15   It is 7:45

Write the time that each clock below shows.

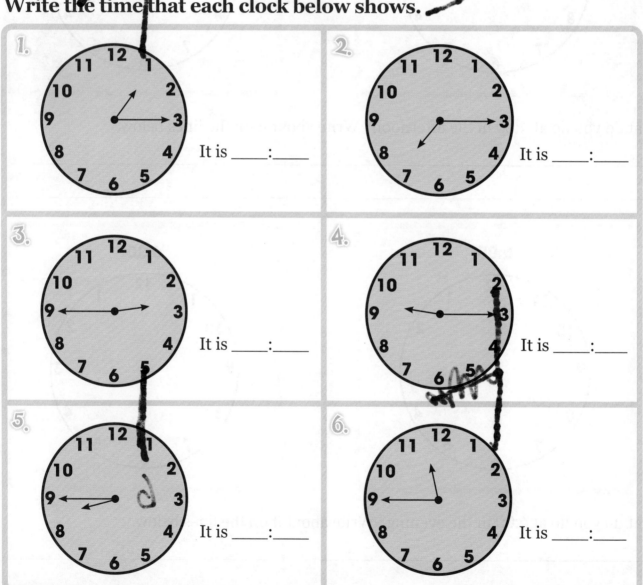

1. It is _____:_____

2. It is _____:_____

3. It is _____:_____

4. It is _____:_____

5. It is _____:_____

6. It is _____:_____

Date: _____

Draw a line to match each time to the correct clock.

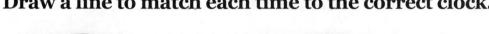

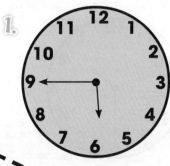

1:45	6:15	2:15

3:45		5:45

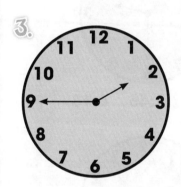

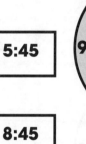

10:15	4:15	8:45

Date: _____

Draw a circle around the correct time under each clock.

1.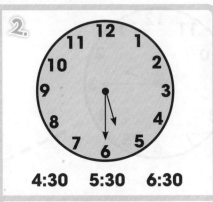

1:00   2:15   1:30

2.

4:30   5:30   6:30

3.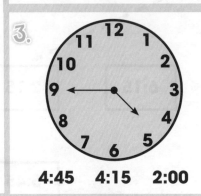

4:45   4:15   2:00

4.

2:30   2:45   6:15

5.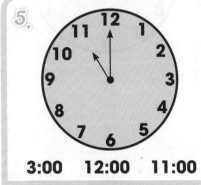

3:00   12:00   11:00

6.

8:30   9:45   3:45

7.

10:15   9:00   10:45

8.

7:00   8:15   8:00

9.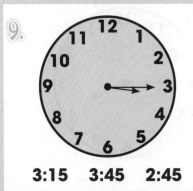

3:15   3:45   2:45

10.

7:15   7:30   7:45

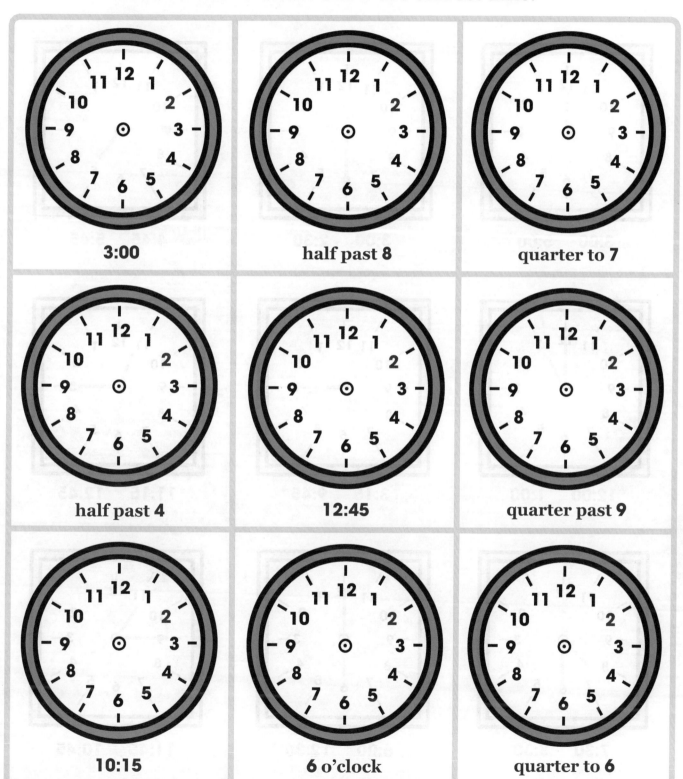

Date: _____

Draw the hands on the clocks to show the correct time.

3:00

half past 8

quarter to 7

half past 4

12:45

quarter past 9

10:15

6 o'clock

quarter to 6

Date: _____

Look at the time shown on the clock face. Circle the correct time.

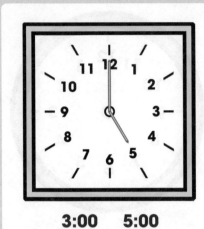

3:00   5:00

3:00   2:30

4:45   5:45

12:00   1:00

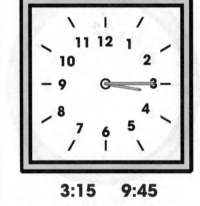

3:15   9:45

11.15   12.45

7:30   8:30

6:00   12:30

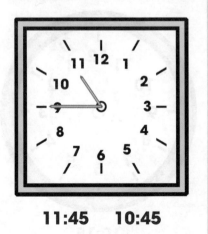

11:45   10:45

Read the riddle. To find the answer, find the clock face that matches the time written under each blank line. Then write the letter under that clock face on the blank line.

What did the little hand on the clock say to the big hand?

"_____ _____ _____ _____ _____ _____ _____
 10:00   3:30   3:30   6:05   2:25   3:45   6:15

_____ _____ _____ _____ _____ _____ !"
 4:45   6:05   2:55   3:45   3:45   2:55

O   U   E   N

T   Y   M   A

Date: _____

Write the time in 3 different ways. The first one has been done for you

1.

   _____7 : 35_____

   ___35___ minutes after ___7___

   ___25___ minutes to ___8___

2.

   _____

   _____ minutes after _____

   _____ minutes to _____

3.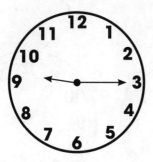

   _____

   _____ minutes after _____

   _____ minutes to _____

4.

   _____

   _____ minutes after _____

   _____ minutes to _____

5.

   _____

   _____ minutes after _____

   _____ minutes to _____

6.

   _____

   _____ minutes after _____

   _____ minutes to _____

Date: _____

Why do we need to know how to tell time? List your ideas below.

_____

_____

_____

_____

How long is a minute? Think about how much you can do in one minute. Write your estimates in the Prediction column. Then time yourself.

Write the actual number in the Result column.

Prediction: In one minute I can	**Result**
Jump rope _____ times.	
Write the numbers 1 to _____.	
Say the names of _____ animals.	

Date: _____

How long does it take to do each action? Circle the correct answer.

1.	Blink eyes	less than 1 min	more than 1 min
2.	Mow a lown	less than 1 min	more than 1 min
3.	Throw a pillow	less than 1 min	more than 1 min
4.	Cycle to school	less than 1 min	more than 1 min
5.	Clap hands once	less than 1 min	more than 1 min
6.	Take a quick shower	less than 1 min	more than 1 min
7.	Swim twenty meters	less than 1 min	more than 1 min
8.	Tie one shoelace	less than 1 min	more than 1 min
9.	Cook rice	less than 1 min	more than 1 min
10.	Jump up and down once	less than 1 min	more than 1 min

Date: _____

How long does it take to do each action? Circle the correct answer.

1.	Wash hair	less than 30 min	more than 30 min
2.	Do the laundry	less than 30 min	more than 30 min
3.	Write the name of your school	less than 30 min	more than 30 min
4.	Walk to the bus stop 2 km away	less than 30 min	more than 30 min
5.	Sing the National Anthem	less than 30 min	more than 30 min
6.	Take a quick shower	less than 30 min	more than 30 min
7.	Drive to school 1 km away	less than 30 min	more than 30 min
8.	Make a sandwich	less than 30 min	more than 30 min
9.	Do a 6-piece puzzle	less than 30 min	more than 30 min
10.	Write the names of all 12 months of the year	less than 30 min	more than 30 min

Date: _____

Write a.m. or p.m.

1.

8 __p.m.__

2.

5:30 __p.m.__

3.

7 __a.m.__

4.

9 __p.m__

Date: _____

Mike's Afternoon Schedule:

12:25	Eat Lunch
1:45	Go to George's House
3:15	Come Home from George's House
5:00	Take a Bath
7:00	Eat Dinner
7:45	Read a Book
8:30	Go to Bed

Write the activity that Mike has planned for each time shown below.

1. Eet dinner

2. Home

3. Lunch

4. Bed

Look at the time shown on the clock faces. Then write how many minutes have passed.

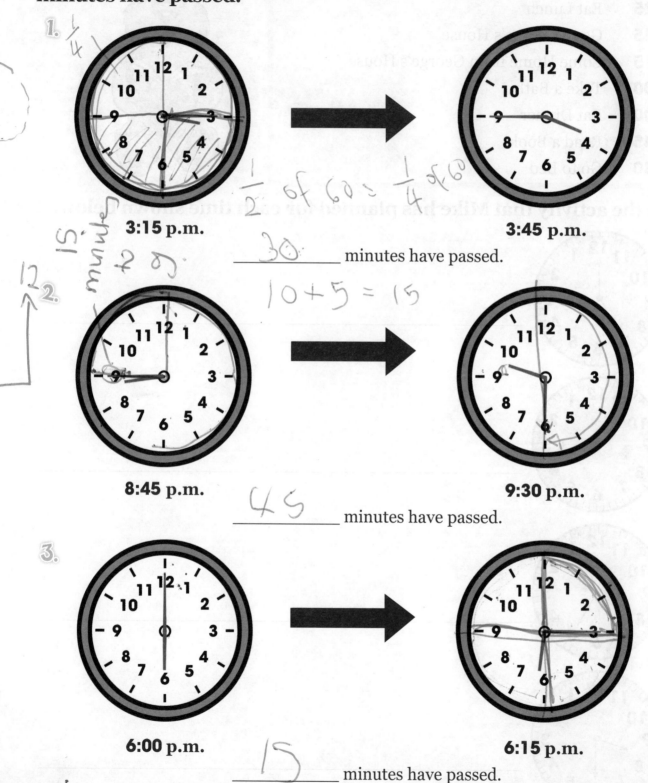

1.

3:15 p.m.

3:45 p.m.

_____30_____ minutes have passed.

10+5 = 15

2.

8:45 p.m.

9:30 p.m.

_____45_____ minutes have passed.

3.

6:00 p.m.

6:15 p.m.

_____15_____ minutes have passed.

Date: _____

Solve the problems.

HOUR

MINUTES

3

1. Henry arrived at the park at 10:15. He flew his kite for 2 hours. What time did he stop flying his kite?

   12 : 15

2. Megan is baking a cake. She put the cake in the oven at 3:02. The directions say to bake the cake for 35 minutes. What time should she take the cake out of the oven?

   3 : 37

3. Mario rode his bike for 3 hours. If he stopped at 5:20, what time did he start?

   2 : 20

4. A train left for Center City at 4:12. The train took 3 hours and fifteen minutes to get to Avon. What time did the train arrive in Avon?

   7 : 27

5. The class recess starts at 1:50 and lasts for 25 minutes. What time does recess end?

   2 : 15

6. Hannah went to the library yesterday. She arrived there at 9:00. She spent 2 hours reading, then spent 20 minutes riding her bike home. What time did she get home?

   11 : 20

Date: _____

Circle the longer object.

1.

(a)

(b)

2.

(a)

(b)

3.

(a)

(b)

Date: _____

Look at the objects. Order them from the shortest to the longest. Write 1 for the shortest length and 3 for the longest length.

1.

2.

3.

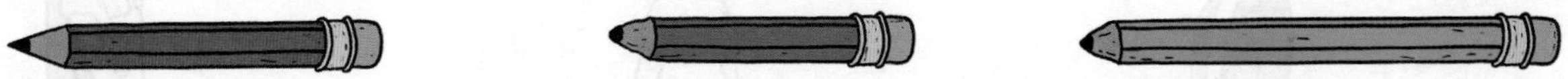

Date: _____

Look at the objects. Order them from the longest to the shortest. Write 1 for the longest length and 3 for the shortest length.

1.

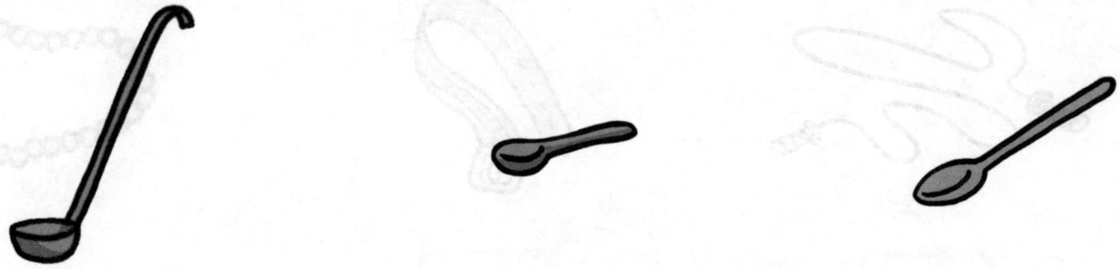

2.

3.

Date: _____

The penguin family is part of the winter parade. They need to line up from the shortest to the tallest. Give them a hand! Use a ruler to measure each penguin. Label each penguin with its height.

Paul	**Peter**	**Patty**	**Petunia**
Height:	Height:	Height:	Height:
_____	_____	_____	_____
cm	cm	cm	cm

Write the name of each penguin in order of their heights, from the shortest to the tallest.

_____   _____   _____   _____

(shortest)   (tallest)

Date: _____

People didn't always measure with rulers. Long ago, Egyptians and other peoples measured objects with body parts. Try it!

1. A "digit" is the width of your index finger at the top joint where it bends. How many digits long is:

   a pair of scissors? _____

   a math book? _____

   a crayon? _____

2. A "palm" is the width of your palm. How many palms long is:

   a telephone book? _____

   your desk? _____

   a ruler? _____

3. A "span" is the length from the tip of your pinkie to the tip of your thumb when your hand is wide open. How many spans long is:

   a broom handle? _____

   a table? _____

   a door? _____

Date: _____

 When measurements need not be exact, lengths can be estimated in non-standard units, such as, with paperclips and the span of the hand.

Measure the following everyday items in non-standard units.

Wooden spoon

Ruler

Eraser

Paperclip

1. The wooden spoon is about _____ rulers long.

2. The ruler is about _____ paperclips long.

3. Two erasers are about _____ paperclips long.

4. Two wooden spoons are about _____ erasers long.

5. The longest object is the _____.

6. The shortest object is the _____.

Date: _____

Length can be measured in **centimeter** *(cm),* **meter** *(m) or* **kilometer** *(km).*
    100 cm = 1 m
    1,000 m = 1 km.

Which unit of measure would you use for the following? Underline the more sensible measure.

How many centimeters to the market, Sir ?

Bus stop

1. Height of a bookcase

   cm   m

2. Width of your backyard

   m   km

3. Length of a river

   m   km

4. Width of a desk

   cm   m

5. Length of your arm

   cm   m

6. Length of a comb

   cm   m

7. Length of a football field

   cm   m

8. Distance from earth to moon

   m   km

9. Depth of a swimming pool

   cm   m

10. Tube of toothpaste

    cm   m

11. Height of a refrigerator

    cm   m

12. Width of a bedroom

    cm   m

13. Distance between 2 cities

    m   km

14. Length of a dollar

    cm   m

15. Length of an automobile

    cm   m

Date: _____

Estimate the length of each ribbon in centimeters (cm). Use a centimeter ruler to check your estimate. Write your answers.

	Estimate	Actual

1.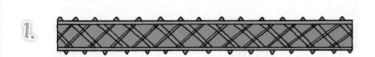

_____ cm _____ cm

2.

_____ cm _____ cm

3.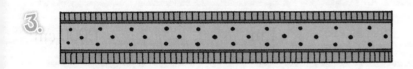

_____ cm _____ cm

4.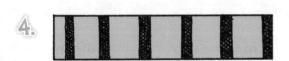

_____ cm _____ cm

5.

_____ cm _____ cm

Cut a 14-centimeter length of paper into three pieces. On the dots, tape the paper from shortest to longest. Measure and write the length of each piece of paper.

• _____ cm

• _____ cm

• _____ cm

Date: _____

Circle the correct estimate for each object.

1.	Length of a bed	2 m	2 cm
2.	Height of a stool	65 m	65 cm
3.	Length of a work bench	92 m	92 cm
4.	Height of a door	2 m	20 cm
5.	Width of a corridor	1 m	1,000 cm
6.	Length of a newborn baby	5 m	50 cm
7.	Length of a car	4 m	40 cm
8.	Width of a Business Class seat	50 m	500 cm
9.	Width of a sink	55 m	55 cm
10.	Length of a basketball court	28 m	280 cm
11.	Height of a street lamp	3 m	30 cm
12.	Width of a car tire	25 m	25 cm

Date: _____

Look at each picture. Estimate how long you think it is. Then measure each picture with a ruler. Write the actual length in centimeters.

	Estimate	Actual

1.

_____ cm   _____ cm

2.

_____ cm   _____ cm

3.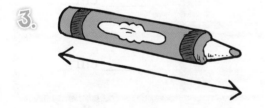

_____ cm   _____ cm

4.

_____ cm   _____ cm

 Practice measuring other things in the room with a ruler.

Date: _____

Find the measurements of the following items.

1.	Measure the length of your foot	_____ cm
2.	Measure your height	_____ cm
3.	Measure your arm span	_____ cm
4.	Measure the width of this page	_____ cm
5.	Measure the thickness of this book	_____ cm
6.	Measure the width of your writing table	_____ cm
7.	Measure the height of a refrigerator	_____ cm
8.	Measure the length of your bath towel	_____ cm
9.	Measure the width of your room door	_____ cm
10.	Measure the height of your chair	_____ cm
11.	Measure the length of a pen	_____ cm
12.	Measure the width of a file	_____ cm

Date: _____

Measure the length of these lines in cm.

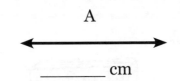

A

_____ cm

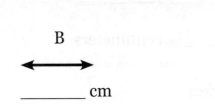

B

_____ cm

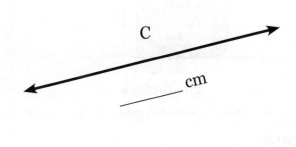

C

_____ cm

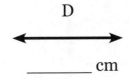

D

_____ cm

How would you measure the length of this string? Explain. Then measure the length of the string.

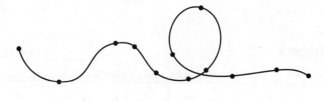

_____

_____

_____

The length of the string is _____ cm long.

Date: _____

Things can be measured using centimeters. Get a ruler that measures in centimeters. Measure the pictures of the objects below.

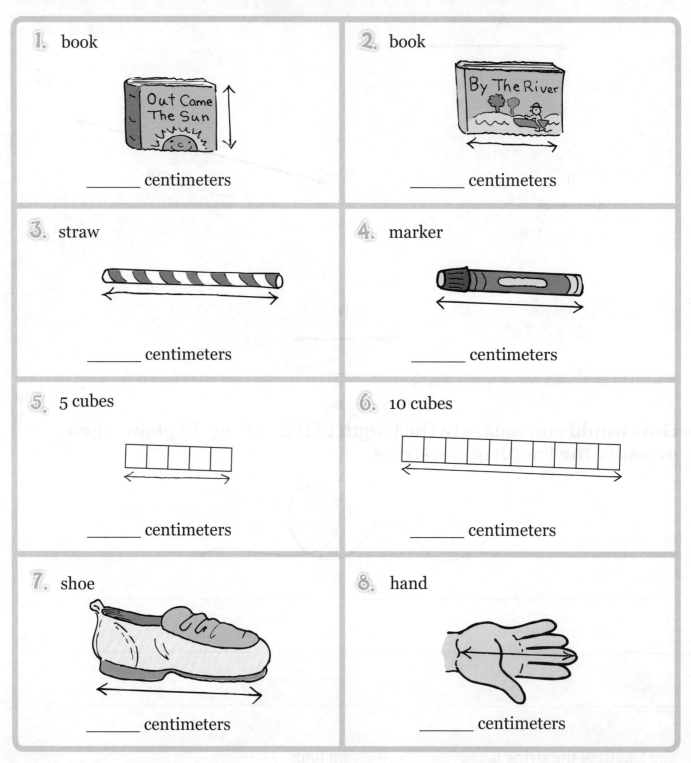

1. book

_____ centimeters

2. book

_____ centimeters

3. straw

_____ centimeters

4. marker

_____ centimeters

5. 5 cubes

_____ centimeters

6. 10 cubes

_____ centimeters

7. shoe

_____ centimeters

8. hand

_____ centimeters

Date: _____

Use a ruler to draw a worm for each length. Remember: one centimeter can also be written as 1 cm.

1. 4 cm long worm

2. 5 cm long worm

3. 8 cm long worm

4. 6 cm long worm

Draw an X in front of each snake that is longer than 7 centimeters.

5.

6.

7.

Date: _____

Use a ruler to measure the line segments. Write your answers in centimeters. Then add to find the total length.

1.

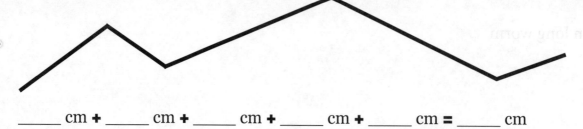

_____ cm + _____ cm + _____ cm + _____ cm + _____ cm = _____ cm

2.

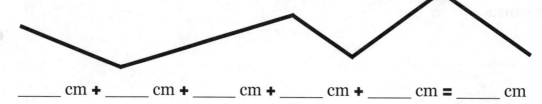

_____ cm + _____ cm + _____ cm + _____ cm + _____ cm = _____ cm

3.

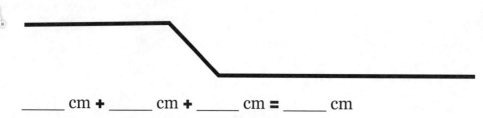

_____ cm + _____ cm + _____ cm = _____ cm

4.

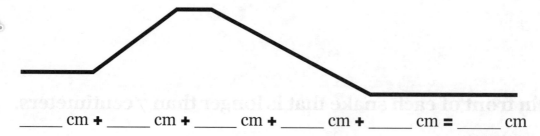

_____ cm + _____ cm + _____ cm + _____ cm + _____ cm = _____ cm

5. Trace the longest line with a red crayon.

(a) _____

(b) _____

(c) _____

6. Trace the shortest line with a blue crayon.

(a) _____

(b) _____

(c) _____

7. Trace the longest line with a green crayon.

(a) (b) (c)

Date: _____

Use the chart to find what size each person wears. Circle your answer.

1. Dale has a 71 cm chest. What size T-shirt does Dale wear?

   Small   Medium   Large

2. Chris has a 68 cm waist. What size shorts does Chris wear?

   Small   Medium   Large

3. Pat wears a 27 cm sandal. What size sandal does Pat wear?

   Small   Medium   Large

4. Cam has a 58 cm waist. What size shorts does Cam wear?

   Small   Medium   Large

5. Sam wears a 10 cm sandal. What size sandal does Sam wear?

   Small   Medium   Large

6. Alex has a 86 cm chest. What size T-shirt does Alex wear?

   Small   Medium   Large

Beachwear-4-U
Size Chart

T-shirts
(chest size)
50 cm–60 cm   Small
61 cm–75 cm   Medium
76 cm–90 cm   Large

Shorts
(waist size)
50 cm–55 cm   Small
56 cm–60 cm   Medium
61 cm–70 cm   Large

Sandals
(shoe size)
10 cm–15 cm   Small
16 cm–22 cm   Medium
23 cm–30 cm   Large

Date: _____

Use a ruler to find the perimeter for each bug box. First, write the number of centimeters that are on each side. Then add all 4 sides together.

1.

_____ + _____ + _____

+ _____ = _____ cm

2.

_____ + _____ + _____

+ _____ = _____ cm

3.

_____ + _____ + _____

+ _____ = _____ cm

4.

_____ + _____ + _____

+ _____ = _____ cm

5.

_____ + _____ + _____

+ _____ = _____ cm

6.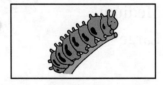

_____ + _____ + _____

+ _____ = _____ cm

7.

_____ + _____ + _____

+ _____ = _____ cm

Date: _____

Use a ruler and measure each side of each rectangle. Write the lengths in the spaces below. Then add up all the sides to find the perimeter or distance, around each rectangle.

1.
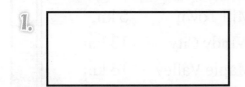

____ + ____ + ____ + ____ = _____ cm

2.

____ + ____ + ____ + ____ = _____ cm

3.
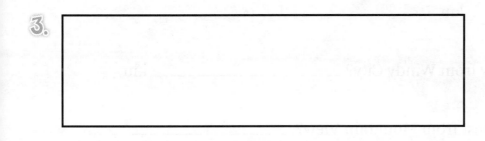

____ + ____ + ____ + ____ = _____ cm

Date: _____

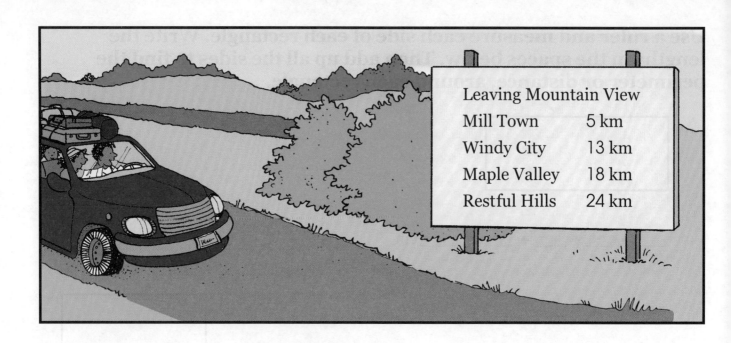

Leaving Mountain View

Mill Town	5 km
Windy City	13 km
Maple Valley	18 km
Restful Hills	24 km

Use the sign to answer the questions.

1. Which town will the family reach next? _____

2. How far away is Mill Town? _____ km

3. Which towns are more than 15 km away now?

   _____ and _____

4. What is the distance between Mill Town and Restful Hills?

   _____ km

5. How far is Maple Valley from Windy City? _____ km

6. Which town is the farthest from Mountain View? _____

Date: _____

Look at the map and distances given below.

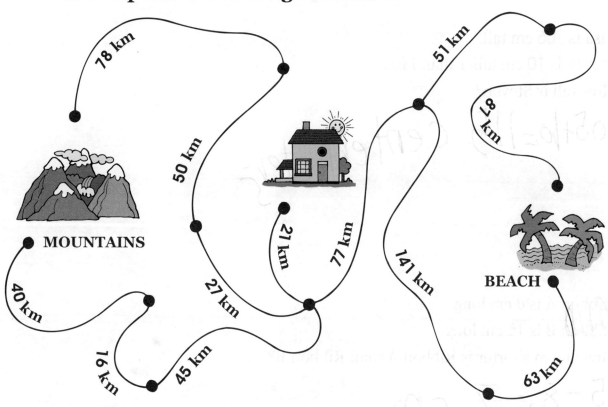

78 km

51 km

87 km

50 km

MOUNTAINS

21 km

77 km

141 km

BEACH

40 km

27 km

16 km

45 km

63 km

---

1. Add the distance of each route from the house to the beach.

	Route 1	Route 2
	_____	_____
	_____	_____
	_____	
+	_____	+ _____
	_____ km	_____ km

2. Add the distance of each route from the house to the mountains.

	Route 1	Route 2
	_____	_____
	_____	_____
	_____	_____
+	_____	+ _____
	_____ km	_____ km

Date: _____

Read the questions. Then solve the problems.

1. Lisa is 105 cm tall.
   Steven is 10 cm taller than Lisa.
   How tall is Steven?

   $105 + 10 = 115$ centermeters

2. Ribbon A is 8 cm long.
   Ribbon B is 15 cm long.
   How much shorter is Ribbon A than Ribbon B?

   $15 - 8 = 7$ cm

3. An eraser is 3 cm long.
   What is the total length of 4 similar erasers?

   $4 \times 3 = 12$ centimetres

Date: _____

Read the questions. Then solve the problems.

1. Emily's house is 1 km away from the library.

   The library is 2 km away from the cinema.

   How far does Emily travel if she goes from her home to the library and then

   to the cinema?

$= 3 \text{ km}$

2. A seamstress needs 100 cm of lace to sew a skirt.

   What length of lace does she need to sew 8 such skirts?

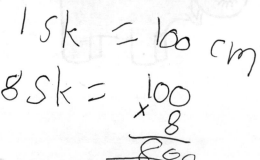

$10 \times 8 = 80$

$100 \times 8 = 800$

$12 - 6 = 6$

$120 - 60 = 60$

3. A mop handle is 60 cm.

   It can be extended to a maximum length of 120 cm.

   What is the difference between the minimum and maximum lengths of

   the mop handle?

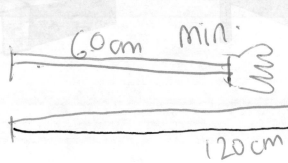

60 cm   min.

max

120 cm

$\begin{array}{r} -120 \\ 60 \\ \hline 60 \text{ cm} \end{array}$

Date: _____

Circle the heavier object.

1.

(a)

(b)

2.

(a)

(b)

3.

(a)

(b)

Date: _____

Circle the lighter object.

1.

a   b

2.

a   b

3.

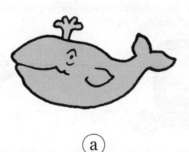 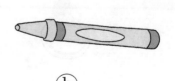

a   b

Date: _____

Look at the objects. Order them from the lightest to the heaviest. Write 1 for the lightest and 3 for the heaviest.

1.

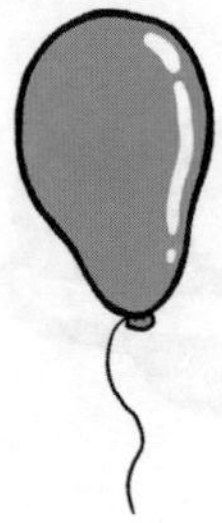

2.

3.

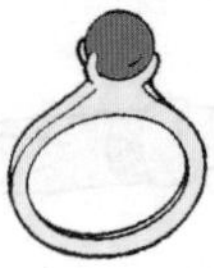

Date: _____

**Look at the objects. Order them from the heaviest to the lightest.
Write 1 for the heaviest and 3 for the lightest.**

1.

2.

3.

Date: _____

Zoey's class went to the zoo. They wrote down how much the animals weighed. Arrange them in weight order — from the lightest to the heaviest.

_____   _____   _____   _____

Seal
150 kg

Lion
162 kg

Deer
100 kg

Bear
241 kg

Date: _____

*Weight can be measured in **grams** (g) and **kilograms** (kg).*
1 kg = 1,000 g.

Which unit of measure would you use to weigh the items below? Underline the more sensible measure.

1. An apple

   grams   kilograms

2. A skateboard

   grams   kilograms

3. A bar of soap

   grams   kilograms

4. A bicycle

   grams   kilograms

5. A watermelon

   grams   kilograms

6. A baseball player

   grams   kilograms

7. A balloon

   grams   kilograms

8. A jam sandwich

   grams   kilograms

9. A baseball bat

   grams   kilograms

10. A pair of socks

    grams   kilograms

11. A slice of pizza

    grams   kilograms

12. A full backpack

    grams   kilograms

13. A large dog

    grams   kilograms

14. A loaf of bread

    grams   kilograms

15. A paintbrush

    grams   kilograms

Date: _____

Read the clues. Use the scales below to help you work out the answer. Then find which object is the lightest.

Object C is heavier than Object A.

Object B is heavier than Object A, but lighter than Object C.

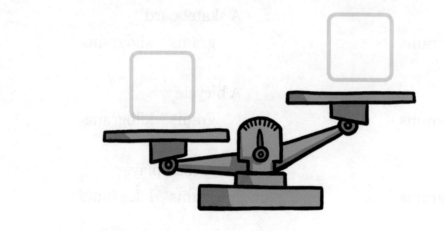

Object _____ is the lightest.

Date: _____

Read the scales. Then work out the problems.

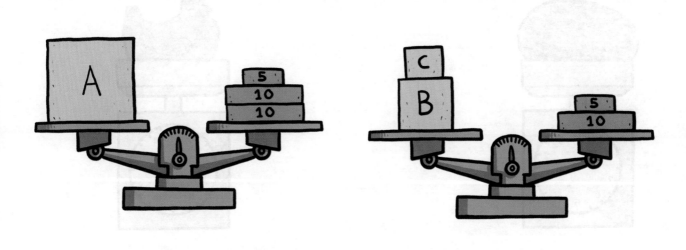

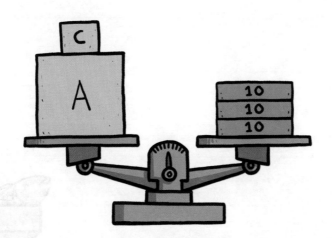

1. Parcel A has a weight of _____ kg.

2. Parcel B has a weight of _____ kg.

3. Parcels A and B have a total weight of _____ kg.

Date: _____

Write the weight of the objects.

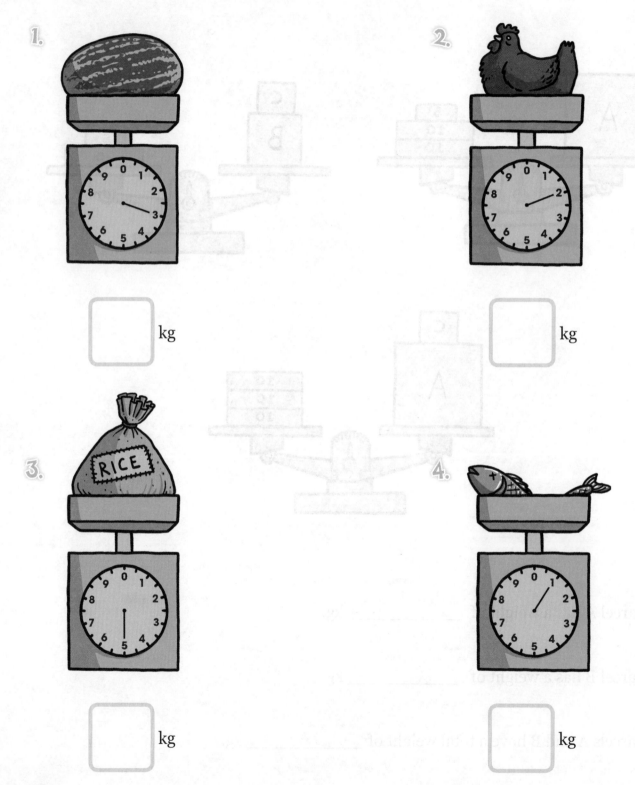

1.

☐ kg

2.

☐ kg

3.

RICE

☐ kg

4.

☐ kg

Date: _____

Write the weight of the objects.

1.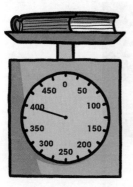

[ ] g

2.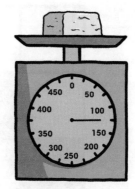

[ ] g

3.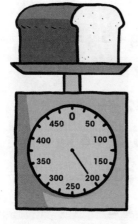

[ ] g

4.

[ ] g

Date: _____

Add or subtract. Write the answer for each question in the puzzle.

Across

1. **4 g + 6 g =**
2. **6 g × 4 =**
3. **36 g – 6 g =**
4. **29 kg – 13 kg =**
5. **325 g – 298 g =**
6. **40 g + 8 g =**
7. **7 kg × 8 =**
9. **40 g + 18 g =**
10. **85 g – 37 g =**

Down

1. **5 g + 5 g + 5 g =**
2. **10 g × 2 =**
3. **78 g – 42 g =**
4. **6 kg + 6 kg + 6 kg =**
5. **56 kg – 30 kg =**
6. **12 kg × 4 =**
8. **413 g – 325 g =**

Date: _____

Read the questions. Then solve the problems.

1.

 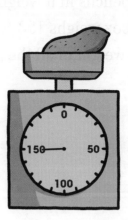

(a) Find the weight of one kiwi fruit. _____ g.

(b) How much lighter is the kiwi fruit than the papaya? _____ g.

2. The weight of one orange is 200 g.
What is the weight of 5 oranges?

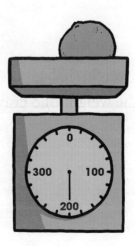

Date: _____

Read the questions. Then solve the problems.

1. A box with pencils in it weighs 864 g.
   The empty box weighs 153 g.
   What is the weight of all the pencils?

2. The weight of a book is 160 g more than the weight of a pen.
   The book is 325 g.
   What is the weight of the pen?

3. A crayon weighs 135 g.
   What is the weight of 8 crayons?

Date: _____

Look at the containers. Which one can hold the most? Circle it. Cross out the container that holds the least.

Date: _____

Look at the pictures below. Circle the set that holds more.

1.

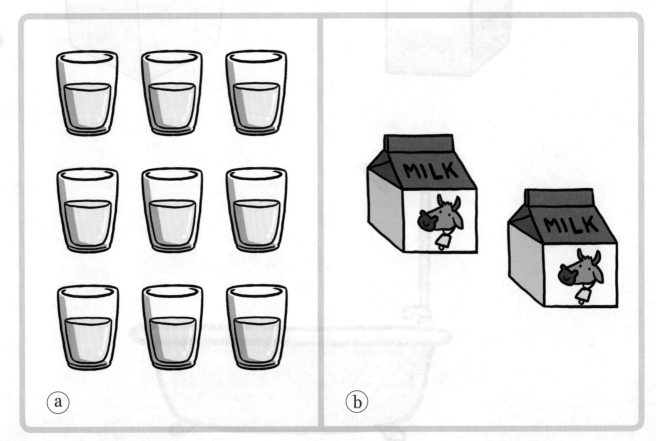

(a)

(b)

Date: _____

Circle the set that holds more.

2.

   ⓐ   ⓑ

3.
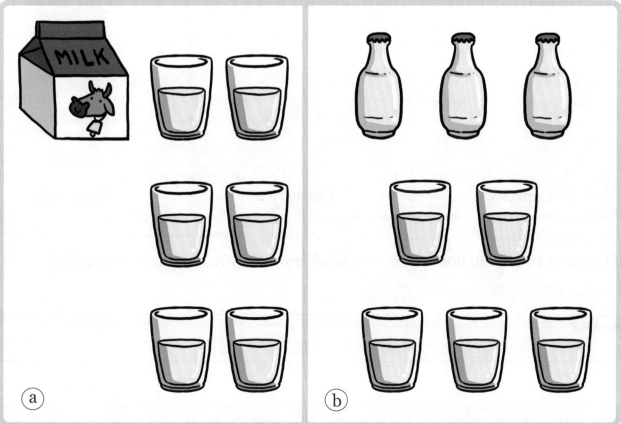

   ⓐ   ⓑ

Date: _____

Look for items around your house that measure content in milliliters or liters. Read the amount of liquid on the label. Then draw the item and record it in the table.

Less than 1 liter	Equal to 1 liter	More than 1 liter
Capacity =	Capacity =	Capacity =
Capacity =	Capacity =	Capacity =

If the item you found does not have a label, how will you measure its capacity?

_____

_____

_____

Date: _____

Look at the pictures. Then answer the questions that follow.

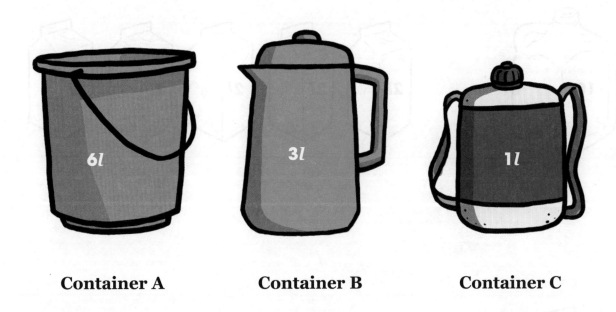

Container A   **Container B**   **Container C**

1. Container _____ holds the most water.

2. Container _____ holds more water than Container _____ but less water than Container _____.

3. Container A is completely filled with water.
    How many Container B are needed to hold all the water from Container A?

Date: _____

How much can each container hold? Color the correct number.

Date: _____

**Find and color the words from the Word Box in the puzzle below.
Words can go diagonally, vertically or horizontally.**

Word Box

centimeter	meter	kilometer
liter	milliliter	hour
minute	kilogram	gram

```
m  e  t  i  r  e  t  l  i  a
l  i  k  i  l  o  g  r  a  m
i  h  l  a  p  r  a  m  o  e
e  o  c  l  e  l  l  t  h  g
c  e  n  t  i  m  e  t  e  r
m  i  e  k  o  l  l  t  k  h
i  m  i  n  t  u  i  o  i  u
n  t  e  r  h  r  t  t  t  o
u  k  i  l  o  m  e  t  e  r
t  e  r  a  u  e  r  e  r  r
e  i  t  g  r  a  m  r  o  h
```

Date: _____

Read the questions. Then solve the problems.

1. A bottle holds 1,000 ml of milk.
   A mug holds 250 ml of milk.
   How many milliliters of milk do both containers hold?

2. There is 330 ml of oil in a bottle.
   Mother pours out 30 ml of oil.
   How much oil is left in the bottle?

3. A cup can hold 220 ml of water.
   A container holds 900 ml of water.
   How many cups can the container of water fill?

Time and Measurement Practice Test

Fill in the bubble next to the correct answer.

1.

What time does the clock show?

- ○ **A** 9:35
- ○ **B** 8:35
- ○ **C** 8:40
- ✓ **D** 8:20

2.

What time does the clock show?

- ✓ **A** 4:10
- ○ **B** 3:10
- ○ **C** 2:00
- ○ **D** 3:20

3.

What time does the clock show?

- ○ **A** 12:05
- ○ **B** 12:55
- ✓ **C** 11:55
- ○ **D** 3:05

4.

What time does the clock show?

- ○ **A** 2:25
- ○ **B** 6:40
- ✓ **C** 1:25
- ○ **D** 5:10

Fill in the bubble next to the correct answer.

5. How many minutes have passed?

- ◯ **A** 1 minute
- ◯ **B** 9 minutes
- ◯ **C** 30 minutes
- ◯ **D** 45 minutes

6. How many minutes have passed?

- ◯ **A** 3 minutes
- ◯ **B** 15 minutes
- ◯ **C** 30 minutes
- ◯ **D** 45 minutes

7. How many minutes have passed?

- ◯ **A** 5 minutes
- ◯ **B** 20 minutes
- ◯ **C** 25 minutes
- ◯ **D** 35 minutes

Time and Measurement
Practice Test

Fill in the bubble next to the correct answer.

Key
● = 1 meter

8. What is the distance between the Umbrella Shop and Beach Toys 4 U?

○ **A** 5 meters

○ **B** 6 meters

○ **C** 7 meters

○ **D** 10 meters

9. What is the distance between the Kite Shop and Aqua Pets?

○ **A** 10 meters

○ **B** 11 meters

○ **C** 12 meters

○ **D** 20 meters

Fill in the bubble next to the correct answer.

10. Which is a better estimate for the length of a bedroom?

○ **A**   6 m

○ **B**   6 CM

○ **C**   6 KG

○ **D**   6 *L*

11. Which is a better estimate for the time taken to jog 2 km?

○ **A**   15 ml

○ **B**   15 km

○ **C**   15 min

○ **D**   15 h

12. Which is a better estimate for the weight of a watermelon?

○ **A**   3 g

○ **B**   3 kg

○ **C**   3 h

○ **D**   3 cm

13. Which is a better estimate for the capacity of a kettle?

○ **A**   5 min

○ **B**   5 kg

○ **C**   5 m

○ **D**   5 *l*

Fill in the bubble next to the correct answer.

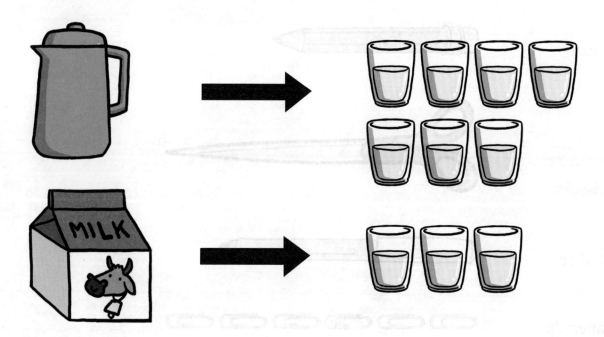

14. How many glasses of water is needed to completely fill two flasks?

- ◯ **A** 3
- ◯ **B** 6
- ◯ **C** 7
- ◯ **D** 14

15. How many more glasses of water can the flask hold than the carton?

- ◯ **A** 3
- ◯ **B** 4
- ◯ **C** 7
- ◯ **D** 10

Fill in the bubble next to the correct answer.

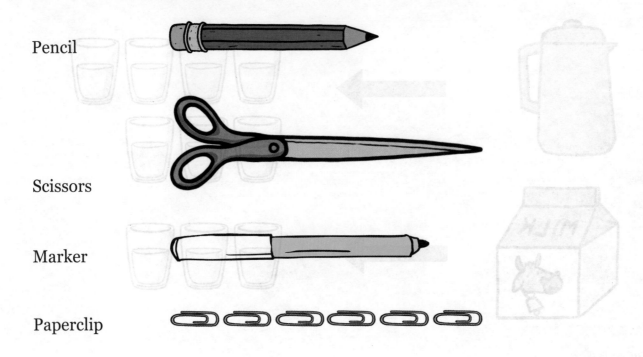

Pencil

Scissors

Marker

Paperclip

16. How much shorter is the pencil than the marker?

○ **A** About 1 paperclip

○ **B** About 5 paperclips

○ **C** About 6 paperclips

○ **D** About 11 paperclips

17. What is the length of the scissors and the marker?

○ **A** About 6 paperclips

○ **B** About 7 paperclips

○ **C** About 12 paperclips

○ **D** About 11 paperclips

Read the questions. Then solve the problems.

18. Mario is making a pizza.
He needs 300 g of cheese to put on a pizza.
He has 145 g of cheese.
How much more cheese does he need?

19. The weight of a pencil is 105 g.
The weight of a book is 365 g.

(a) What is the weight of 3 pencils?

(b) What is the weight of 3 pencils and 1 book?

Time and Measurement Practice Test

Read the questions. Then solve the problems.

20. Suresh stopped playing football at 8:20 p.m.

He played for 30 minutes.

At what time did he start to play football?

21. Kimberly drank 10l of water on Monday.

She drank 3l less on Tuesday.

(a) How much water did she drink on Tuesday?

(b) How much water did she drink in total on both days?

Answer Key

Page 6
3 o'clock, 2 o'clock, 12 o'clock,
8 o'clock, 6 o'clock, 11 o'clock,
1 o'clock, 5 o'clock, 9 o'clock

Page 7
4 o'clock or 4:00, 11 o'clock or 11:00,
8 o'clock or 8:00, 2 o'clock or 2:00,
6 o'clock or 6:00, 10 o'clock or 10:00,
7 o'clock or 7:00, 1 o'clock or 1:00,
5 o'clock or 5:00

Page 8
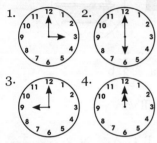

Page 9
half past 1,   half past 6,   half past 10,
half past 8,   half past 3,   half past 12,
half past 5,   half past 9,   half past 2

Page 10
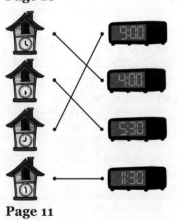

Page 11
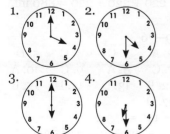

Review answers

Page 12
1. 1:15   2. 7:15   3. 2:45
4. 9:15   5. 8:45   6. 11:45

Page 13
1. 5:45   2. 4:15   3. 1:45   4. 6:15
5. 8:45   6. 3:45   7. 10:15

Page 14
Circle: 1. 1:30   2. 5:30   3. 4:45
4. 2:30   5. 11:00   6. 9:45   7. 10:15
8. 8:00   9. 3:15   10. 7:30

Page 15

Page 16
Circle: 5:00,   2:30,   4:45,   1:00,
3:15,   11:15,   7:30,   6:00,   10:45

Page 17
"MEET YOU AT NOON!"

Page 18
1. 7:35, 35 minutes after 7,
   25 minutes to 8
2. 3:50, 50 minutes after 3,
   10 minutes to 4
3. 9:15, 15 minutes after 9,
   45 minutes to 10
4. 6:25, 25 minutes after 6,
   35 minutes to 7
5. 9:55, 55 minutes after 9,
   5 minutes to 10
6. 2:05, 5 minutes after 2,
   55 minutes to 3

Page 19
Answers will vary.

Page 20
1. less than   2. more than
3. less than   4. more than
5. less than   6. more than
7. more than   8. less than
9. more than   10. less than

Page 21
1. less than   2. more than
3. less than   4. more than
5. less than   6. less than
7. less than   8. less than
9. less than   10. less than

Page 22
1. 8 p.m.   2. 5.30 p.m.
3. 7 a.m.   4. 9 p.m.

Page 23
1. Eat Dinner
2. Come Home from George's House
3. Eat Lunch   4. Go to Bed

Page 24
1. 30 minutes   2. 45 minutes
3. 15 minutes

Pages 25
1. 12:15   2. 3:37   3. 2:20
4. 7:27   5. 2:15   6. 11:20

Page 26
Circle: 1. b   2. a   3. b

Page 27
1. 3, 2, 1   2. 1, 3, 2   3. 2, 1, 3

Page 28
1. 1, 3, 2   2. 1, 3, 2   3. 3, 2, 1

Page 29
9 cm, 5 cm, 4 cm, 8 cm;
Patty, Peter, Petunia, Paul

Page 30
Answers will vary.

Page 31
1. 2   2. 3   3. 3   4. 8
5. wooden spoon   6. paperclip

Page 32
1. cm   2. m   3. km   4. cm   5. cm
6. cm   7. m   8. km   9. m   10. cm
11. m   12. m   13. km   14. cm   15. m

Page 33
Review all estimates.
Actual: 1. 8 cm   2. 5 cm   3. 9 cm
4. 6 cm   5. 7 cm; Review that
directions have been followed.

Page 34
1. 2 m   2. 65 cm   3. 92 cm
4. 2 m   5. 1 m   6. 50 cm
7. 4 m   8. 500 cm   9. 55 cm
10. 28 m   11. 3 m   12. 25 cm

Page 35
Review all estimates.
Actual: 1. 6 cm   2. 4 cm   3. 5 cm
4. 3 cm

Page 36
Answers will vary.

Page 37
A: 4 cm, B: 2 cm, C: 7 cm, D: 3 cm;
Answers will vary;
The string is 15 cm long.

Page 38
1. 2 cm   2. 3 cm   3. 5 cm   4. 4 cm
5. 3 cm   6. 6 cm   7. 5 cm   8. 3 cm

Page 39
1–4. Review that worms of exact
lengths are drawn.
X should be drawn on snake 5 and
snake 7

Page 40
1. 3 cm + 2 cm + 5 cm + 5 cm +
   2 cm = 17 cm
2. 3 cm + 5 cm + 2 cm + 3 cm +
   3 cm = 16 cm
3. 4 cm + 2 cm + 7 cm = 13 cm
4. 2 cm + 3 cm + 1 cm + 5 cm +
   4 cm = 15 cm
5. a   6. c   7. a

Page 41
1. Medium   2. Large   3. Large
4. Medium   5. Small   6. Large

Page 42
1. 3 + 3 + 3 + 3 = 12 cm
2. 4 + 4 + 4 + 4 = 16 cm
3. 4 + 3 + 4 + 3 = 14 cm
4. 2 + 1 + 2 + 1 = 6 cm
5. 1 + 1 + 1 + 1 = 4 cm
6. 4 + 2 + 4 + 2 = 12 cm
7. 1 + 4 + 1 + 4 = 10 cm

Page 43
1. 2 + 5 + 2 + 5 = 14 cm
2. 4 + 7 + 4 + 7 = 22 cm
3. 3 + 11 + 3 + 11 = 28 cm

Page 44
1. Mill Town   2. 5 km
3. Maple Valley and Restful Hills

4. 19 km   5. 5 km
6. Restful Hills

Page 45
1. Route 1. 21 + 77 + 51 + 87 = 236
   Route 2. 21 + 77 + 141 + 63 = 302
2. Route 1. 21 + 27 + 50 + 78 = 176
   Route 2. 21 + 45 + 16 + 40 = 122

Page 46
1. 105 + 10 = 115 cm
2. 15 − 8 = 7 cm   3. 3 × 4 = 12 cm

Page 47
1. 1 + 2 = 3 km
2. 100 × 8 = 800 cm
3. 120 − 60 = 60 cm

Page 48
1. a   2. b   3. b

Page 49
1. b   2. a   3. b

Page 50
1. 2, 1, 3   2. 2, 1, 3   3. 1, 3, 2

Page 51
1. 3, 2, 1   2. 2, 3, 1   3. 3, 1, 2

Page 52
Deer, Seal, Lion, Bear

Page 53
1. grams   2. kilograms
3. grams   4. kilograms
5. kilograms   6. kilograms
7. grams   8. grams
9. kilograms   10. grams
11. grams   12. kilograms
13. kilograms   14. grams
15. grams

Page 54
Object A is the lightest.

Page 55
1. 25 kg   2. 10 kg   3. 35 kg

Page 56
1. 3 kg   2. 2 kg   3. 5 kg   4. 1 kg

Page 57
1. 400 g   2. 125 g   3. 200 g   4. 60 g

Page 58

Page 59
1. ⓐ 35 + 35 = 70 g
   ⓑ 150 − 35 = 115 g
2. 200 × 5 = 1,000 g

Page 60
1. 864 − 153 = 711 g
2. 325 − 160 = 165 g
3. 135 + 135 + 135 + 135 + 135 +
   135 + 135 + 135 = 1,080 g

Page 61

Page 62–63
1. a   2. a   3. b

Page 64
Answers will vary.

Page 65
1. A   2. B, C, A   3. 2

Page 66
Row 1: Color 5 cartons
Row 2: 2 small cartons
Row 3: 10 spoons

Page 67
m	e	t	i	r	e	t	l	i	a
l	i	k	i	l	o	g	r	a	m
i	h	l	a	p	r	a	m	o	e
e	o	c	e	l	l	t	h	g	r
c	e	n	t	i	m	e	t	e	r
m	i	e	k	o	l	t	k	h	u
i	m	i	n	t	u	l	i	o	o
n	t	e	r	h	r	i	t	t	r
u	k	i	l	o	m	e	t	e	r
t	e	r	a	u	e	r	e	r	r
e	i	t	g	r	a	m	r	o	h

Page 68
1. 1,000 + 250 = 1,250 ml
2. 330 − 30 = 300 ml
3. 220 + 220 + 220 + 220 = 880 ml,
   4 cups

Page 69–76
1. D   2. A   3. C   4. C   5. D
6. B   7. C   8. A   9. C   10. A
11. C   12. B   13. D   14. D   15. B
16. A   17. D
18. 300 − 145 = 155 g
19. ⓐ 105 + 105 + 105 = 315 g
    ⓑ 315 + 365 = 680 g
20. 7:50 p.m.
21. ⓐ 7 *l*   ⓑ 17 *l*

Learning Express

Congratulations!

I, _____Ella_____

am a Scholastic Superstar!

Paste a photo or draw a
picture of yourself.

KidS I have completed Time and Measurement L2.

are ybr obRm $

Presented on _____Ella_____

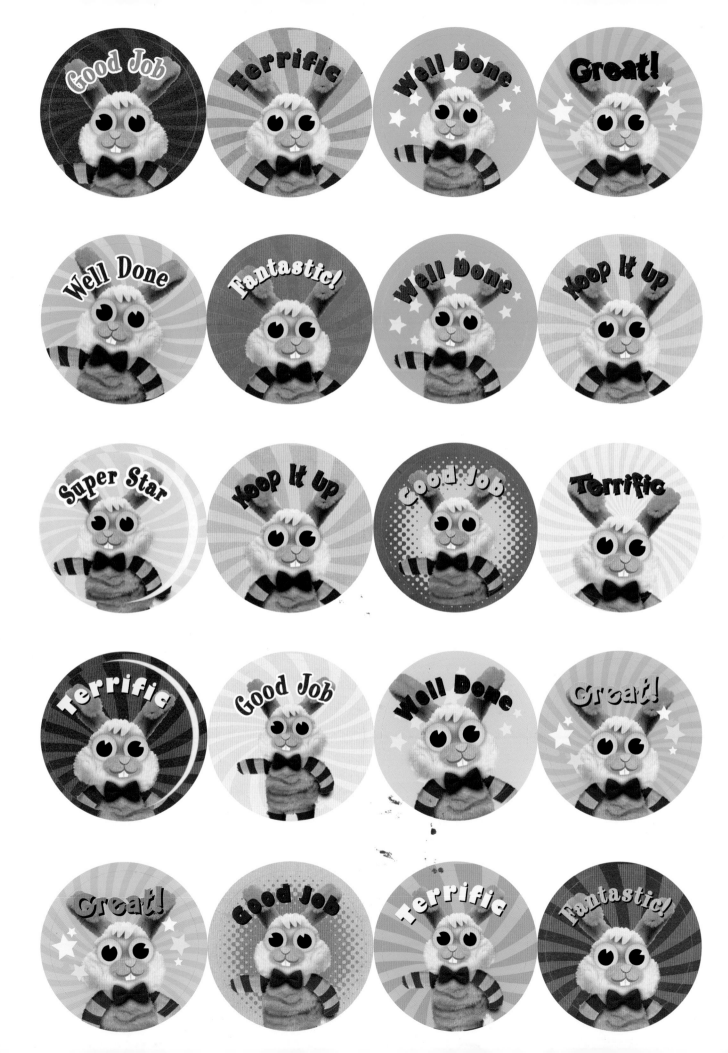